This book is dedicated to all the tough moments, rough
patches, betrayals, heartbreaks, and devastation that each of
us walks through in this short life. The light that comes from
this pain in knowing that no one person is alone in their walk
through this darkness, that light is dedicated to my Dad.
Because in my darkest hour, my passion was ignited and that
flame has inspired me to push through my fear and bring me
to where I am in the present. Thank you Dad for always
pushing me even after you were gone.
I love you.

CONTENTS

INTRODUCTION

The Perfect Plan

Just when you think you have it all figured out….splat! There goes your perfect little ice cream dream. It's so funny because that is honestly how life works out sometimes; doesn't always mean it's bad, but doesn't always mean it's good either.

The cover for this photo and the debacle that unfolded as it was being created could not be any more fitting for this book. We were in LA and had rented a studio for an hour, my best friend and I had a plan. The perfect plan. She was modeling for the photo and she was going to stand there with the ice cream cone and have a smile on her beautiful face and her pup was going to sit there, perfectly still and the ice cream was going to maintain its perfect form for the perfect cover shot, while I captured the absolute perfect angle…. but as we all know, nothing ever really goes according to plan.

Amidst me having no idea what I was doing as far as photography goes, us trying to setup the scene, her dog wanting to lay down and lick up all the little ice cream driblets, my friend, who is an extremely talented model, was working against all odds to try and get her dog to face the right direction while still posing magically. Her boyfriend was frantically making ice cream runs down the street in LA traffic, which by the time it got to the studio, was melting in dramatic fashion. We were down to ten minutes to get the right photo.

While I was pondering all my options and the ice cream continued to melt everywhere, my bestie decided to just drop it on the canvas. At first, I had a minor heart attack as I looked at my last sweet hope of photo redemption hit the floor. But then, her and I looked at each other and it was seriously the most perfect splat I had ever seen. I'm not kidding. If a splat could be perfect, this was it. I started snapping pictures, we ate some of the ice cream, well what was left of it, and we wrapped up the shoot.

That moment was just a blip in life, but it taught me a very important lesson that I'm sure most of us can relate to. No matter how much we plan or how perfect our plans may be, there is always going to be the unpredictable, the unforeseen, the variable we forgot to consider. And even though it may get messy and we may not understand in the moment, things tend to work out in the end. It's not in spite of bad things or circumstances that you fulfill your dreams, it's because of those things. They allow us to develop the skills and character we need in order to become who we are meant to be.

I know I am meant to share my stories through poetry, it gives my emotions purpose, so I genuinely hope this book of poems can be as therapeutic to read as it was to write.

Love you all,

Breathe You In

I wake and see you smile,
your face moves to accommodate its grace.
Your eyes follow mine for awhile,
our bodies moving in, to close the space.

I tuck my nose into your neck.
I breathe as deep as my lungs allow.
My eyes notice every particle and speck,
my lips take in the sweet taste of now.

Trying to soak up this moment I yearn,
every part of the present this is.
A gift I have no desire to return,
I embrace every second I'm his.

The way he sees right through my mind
looking deeply into my eyes and heart,
he knows behind every expression he'll find,
a love beyond what either could part.

Shattered Dreams

If a shattered dream could break further,
it would reveal a shattered heart.
If a shattered dream could inflict pain,
I honestly couldn't even tell you where to start.

For what once was believed to be true,
has now become lost and completely empty.
It has transformed into a colorless hue,
a raw wound that burns when even touched gently.

No matter the strength for which we push thoughts out,
or the mask we wear to facilitate the facade,
the flashes of what was seen no doubt,
burn deep as we try to turn to God.

At times it can be hard to rise out of bed,
the weight of sadness throwing me down.
At times it seems I'd rather be dead,
my heart can no longer handle what can never be found.

How can you ever move on from this ache?
It consumes every fiber in my being, my mind, and my soul.
How can you forgive one who leaves devastation in his wake,
one who seems to care less regarding his role.

If only we could turn back time and try to rewind,
we do the what if, but if, I did that, and changed this,
but it's just a futile attempt of the mind,
in finding a way to justify the chaos amiss.

Each day brings a new struggle to light.
A memory, a motion, an object, a touch.
The gut wrenching and twisting of the night,
allows no rest as the dreams remind us so much.

You think about what could've been,
the adventures that never made it beyond a plan.
Your face drenched in endless tears again,
how could you have fallen for this man?

As the days move to weeks and you no longer dread the hour,
you'll start to see the lesson learned, the silver lining.
You'll begin to seek the beautiful; the positive amidst the sour.
You start to write poems, they help with all they're rhyming.

A small light might be seen in the depths of the sea,
a small glimpse that things can still flow with grace.
Your heart yearns to finally be
Far, far away from this dark and lonely place.

So it's possible for a shattered dream to break, to weep,
each piece like a dagger into the broken heart below.
It's possible for the pain inflicted to run deep,
More deep than we could ever know.

Vacation From my Mind

Unlike a beautiful, private island,
the mind can be a quite hectic place.
Despite the grooves and sensitive linings,
the mind can be a dangerous space.

It never stops thinking and analyzing and categorizing.
It never stops listing and chatting and creating while
delegating.
It never stops firing and feeling and moving amidst
connecting.
It never stops to just let me sit still without debating.

The sand on an island is soft, trickling slowly between your
toes.
The sand in my mind is simply time in an hour glass,
reminding me my age and things I have yet to do,
things I have yet to see, yet to be, trickling, it won't last.

Instead of soaking in the sun and basking in it's warmth,
I feel I am burning up without any protection.
There's no shade, just constant heat and pressure.
Each ray searing my skin, reminding me of pain, all the
imperfection.

Normally the warm water would wash ashore, leaving shells
in its wake,
as it retracts the sand moves slowly under your feet,
but this water that is my mind flows in a frigid way,
revealing sharp coral within its domain and no oasis from the
heat.

The waves can be a soothing sound, not unlike a lullaby,
but the waves crashing against my head never end,
They keep pounding relentlessly until addressed,
My mind, my mind is anything but a calming friend.

So when people say they need a vacation from their vacation,
I truly do understand this meaning in a different way.
The vacation from my mind would truly be a vacation,
name the price, I'd be happy to pay.

Addict Addiction

What happens when your love for something turns,
it becomes the opposite of original intention.
What happens when your love for someone burns,
it becomes a wound that needs serious attention.

What happens when your love for something goes crazy,
it becomes a bad habit that needs more.
What happens when your love for someone gets hazy,
it becomes confusing, exhausting, painful to the core.

What happens when your person starts to change,
it becomes something it can not stand.
What happens when it destroys everything in range,
it becomes destruction, disappointment, ruin at hand.

What happens when your person is someone else,
they become unrecognizable to your loving eyes.
What happens when you lose control of self,
you become entangled in their web of lies.

What happens when you cry because they cry,
you transform into the person they need you to be.
What happens when you die because they die,
what kind of life is this for you to lead?

What kind of life can you expect to have,
if all you do is what they need.
What kind of life are you giving up,
if all you do is grieve, plead, and bleed.

The toughest part is watching the inflicted,
it's letting go when it's time.
When the addict becomes addicted,
the life wasted is the true crime.

Who I am is Grateful

Who is this person, fighting through the trials,
I feel I know her flowing soul.
The lines around her laughs and smiles,
the pain and hurt that played their role.

There is so much that remains the same,
but even more that has quite changed.
Is it possible to know your heart,
but at the moment, feel estranged?

I have tired from all the lessons being taught,
each person teaching something new.
I have learned more than I ever thought,
I have loved and lost quite a few.

When I stare deep into the darkest place
there's something familiar I can see.
I keep looking and looking at my face,
how did this person come to be.

I really can't take all the credit,
I'll give the credit where it's due.
I am grateful, there I said it.
I'll tell you why, in a word or two.

I'm grateful for the verbal abuse,
the controlling nature he exerted.
It taught me to be recluse,
stand up, say my piece, be assertive.

I'm grateful for the stalking time,
living in fear with every turn.
It taught me the true meaning of a crime,
It's important that I learned.

I'm grateful for the lazy one,
who always started but never finished.
It taught me that what's done is done,
our love had finally, truly diminished.

I'm grateful for the perpetual liar,
he really had me going.
It taught me to always aim much higher,
and that even I can't be all knowing.

I'm grateful for the moment ensnared,
the assault on my body and mind.
It taught me that no matter how prepared,
there are people who are not so very kind.

I'm grateful for the trust-less divorcee,
oh the fires I had to put out.
It taught me the value of patience all day,
he needed more time, there is no doubt.

I'm grateful for the military man,
he never showed too much emotion.
It taught me that I can only do what I can,
you can't force someone into devotion.

I'm grateful for the cheating bastard,
Who tore my heart in half.
It taught me that age cannot be mastered,
And that addictions are no laugh.

There are plenty others I am grateful for,
I truly cherish what I'm given.
I take each piece and welcome more,
they're part of me and this life I'm livin.

Empty Bottle

It stares back at me,
no remorse in its wake.
It laughs at me,
mocking everything at stake.

It seems so easy to just
deny the desire,
but for those who must,
the cravings get higher and higher.

Those around you keep hoping
or they finally give up.
It's the only way for coping,
grab the bottle, toss the cup.

The Peace We Seek

Like a phoenix from the ashes,
there is rebirth after the burn.
With all due time so it passes,
and then the heart, it begins to yearn.

Like a moth drawn to the light,
we will emerge from the dark.
We will fly throughout the night,
until we come upon a spark.

Like the penguin that awaits his wife,
so we stand here filled with hope.
All we have is this one life,
and it can be a slippery slope.

Like the fawn that is just born,
so we struggle to stand upright.
We fall, and fall, and fall some more,
but we will never stop the fight.

Like the monk who quiets his mind,
so we soon will find some peace.
We can leave it all behind,
we can find what we surely seek.

And then one day like a child,
we feel pure joy for all to see.
The past is past and reconciled,
what is meant to be will be.

New Caress

For the moment it feels existential.
As I lay here, my breath is calm.
My thoughts surround the potential,
as your hand caresses my palm.

I breath even more fully.
I think back to what was before.
Had it been like this initially?
No matter, because it is no more.

It truly is the break of a new dawn,
all I care about is the present.
The past has come and gone,
I will not let myself be hesitant.

You have breached my thoughts at a new level,
reached over and under my strong wall.
Our conversations surround the credible,
the creative, the mythological, we talk about it all.

How can I possibly feel this excited?
Am I diving in head first?
My soul, my love, my life ignited,
the water to finally quench my thirst.

The moment I truly felt what's here,
was on the pillow of your chest.
I slowly saw your fire, no fear,
I could finally lay my head to rest.

Only a few days have passed us by.
Am I just a silly fool craving what I lack?
Am I raising you up too high,
I fear that where I am, I can't go back.

It reminds me of that cold ball of white,
you roll and roll as it gets bigger.
You pack that snow ever so tight,
once you start, you let go of the trigger.

The bullet is propelled into the air,
there is the inevitable impact.
You hope that whatever is there,
the rocks allow to stay intact.

For as the tumbling motion begins,
the avalanche won't stop.
The crazy ride of love is unhinged,
the roller coaster reaches the top.

Once you take the loop around,
the wheels remain on course,
You pray that when you hit the ground,
it will be by choice and not remorse.

I will say this with no regret,
I choose to love, despite the rest.
I will simply hit reset,
I will embrace this new caress.

My Gem's Gem

You my dear are the rarest of gems,
you're bluer than the bluest of sapphires.
You have been there more than all of the friends,
you have helped me sniff out all the liars.

You have been my rock when my heart is sand,
falling to pieces in the ocean of life.
You have been there holding my hand,
when others' words have cut like a knife.

I would move across states to simply be near,
as our parents very well know.
You have been so kind in lending your ear,
when I didn't know which direction to go.

Your kindness overflows from your cup,
I really don't know how you do it.
You have taught me to never give up,
no matter what, we will simply get through it.

To finally see you happier beyond belief,
gives me more joy than you will ever know.
You deserve the best, what a relief,
you have a man who will never let you go.

Floating

I am but a small object floating on the water,
the form I take is insignificant, like my story.
I am not sinking or drowning nor do I totter,
I simply exist on land and sea in all my glory.

For my purpose has been lost as I've searched,
for what I seek I do not even know.
I wish I could put how I feel in words, but I'd besmirch
the life I attempted to create and grow.

I simply exist, not even attempting to swim,
as I cross by land after land nearby.
I wish I could feel anything but empty and dim,
my light has faded against the evening sky.

Can each day truly be new if you feel the same,
each movement, every love, the work, the thoughts.
My passion has passed, my fluidity lame.
If I escape, can true passion be retaught.

Trying to do more than float, trying to rise above,
how can one appear to have it all but actually nothing.
How can one feel so much feel and love all the love
But return to their home amongst internal suffering.

But to no avail, here I am, I just am, soulless and dying,
reaching for something to lead me away.
My skills and potential attempting to escape and crying,
reaching for nothing as I float, yet another day.

Dandelion

Like whispers in the wind,
small pieces of the dandelion
float casually and as they descend,
I see the passing day sighing.

How small and insignificant this
life is showing me the flightiness
that is the present abyss,
the world pulling with its mightiness.

How the wind is like the waves,
me a speck of sand lost with the rest.
Each roll of the wave craves
more and more of the nothing I possess.

And here even in nature it's evident,
despite the beauty, the torture within.
We are but a simple number, time lent,
energy recycled, longing to be used but when.

We grasp and reach for what we can't.
Always searching but never found.
The dissatisfaction with life a rant,
lost in the wind, no sound.

My Angel

I know you see into the depths,
my soul that has no bound.
My sadness covered by a smile inept,
before you, I had not been found.

Who knew angels came in your form.
You bring out the adventurous,
the dreaming, the longing, a perfect storm,
the playful, the joy, the curiousness.

Because I don't know what life was before you.
I simply live for you,
I implore you,
my Angel, I adore you.

What It Seems

When we glance in the mirror,
the things we say and what we see,
the desire to constantly restore,
what is no more.

To rewind time and recover what's lost
is something for the future, ironic.
The things we become,
to desire freedom.

Trapped is what comes to mind,
confined to these walls staring at me.
Forever longing a feeling,
forever hitting the ceiling.

What it seems,
are only dreams.

To Feel

Anything at all brings nothing,
my emptiness like a gaping hole.
Throw whatever in, simply stuffing,
trying to revive my dying soul.

The tender misery that dwells
has lived so long that we're acquainted.
Any happiness it quells,
turned away, as if it's tainted.

What once was can be no more,
too much experience and time has passed.
To feel something, anything, I implore,
this emptiness can't last.

The Mask

A mask is many colors,
it can elicit many things.
It can fool all the others,
but you know it only brings,

a forbidden love forgiven,
a sadness unseen,
a smile simply hidden,
a painted face unclean.

Personalities untrue,
the necessity to hide.
Wouldn't you rather be you,
so people can see inside.

Count on Me

I can always count on you to push me,
beyond where I'd normally try to go.
I can always see things logically
because that's your method to help me grow.

I definitely get my stubborn nature
straight from your endless source.
I definitely get your sense of humor,
which terrifies me the most of course.

You are without a doubt,
the smartest person that I know.
Despite my unique and newfound route,
you are always there to support my goal.

Even when I didn't want to hear
the words I need to hear the most,
your words of wisdom make it clear,
that life is not a piece of toast.

You taught me the value of a hard days work,
that all things come with a price.
You taught me tenacity with a smirk,
you taught me to lead and not think twice.

I owe my handyman skills to you,
as painful as that process tended to be.
Those are but just a few,
the life lessons you gave to me.

You trusted me with all your fish,
to this day I am not sure why.
I tend to wander, dream and wish,
but still you were always on my side.

And now to think you are leaving,
is devastating to my core.
For awhile I'll be grieving,
if we could talk, just once more.

Just Thoughts

The thought of an aimless isle,
the thought of dancing all alone,
the thought of facing all life's trials,
the thought of doing it on my own.

The thought of a ring without permission,
the thought of losing all security,
the thought of a ticket with no admission,
the thought of a movie with no impurity.

The thought of all the tools in the box,
the thought of all the guns astray,
the thought of skipping without any rocks,
the thought of a week without the day.

The thought of coasting with no flight,
the thought of a captain with no boat,
the thought of another sleepless night,
the thought of watching TV with no remote.

The thought of everything different than you think,
the thought of taking life for granted,
the thought of toasting without a drink,
the thought of dealing with what we're handed.

The thought of seeing you in that bed,
the thought of thoughts tumbling with me,
the thought of things that were unsaid,
the thought of you drifting out to sea.

My Captain

And like a boat with no captain,
no light to find the shore,
I drift amongst an ocean of grief,
helplessly wishing for times no more.

Wave upon wave consumes my soul,
my heart shattered like broken shells.
My father, my hero, my captain,
he is gone, I love you, I miss you, farewell.

Drifting Away

Saying goodbye is more than heart breaking,
especially to a great dad and husband.
The best brother and son, not an easy undertaking,
our hearts will forever be on the mend.

We love and appreciate you more than you'll ever know.
Allowing us life and laughter in abundance.
Always there for learning and lessons, helping us grow,
shaping our minds, giving us good sense.

But now as we cruise amongst the waves,
memories, stories and sadness flood our minds.
We leave you with the ocean, a peaceful place,
though we will never truly leave you behind.

Always around us.
Always guiding.
Always with us.

We love you.

Pain's Cure

I'm trying not to hate God or his plan,
for what he's taken is irreplaceable.
For what he's taken is the only man,
who can do the job he was placed here for.

The pain and suffering I endure,
will only continue to grow as days go on.
Some say time can be a cure,
but there is no remedy for what is gone.

Monsters

The emotions are like a whirlwind of destruction,
my heart and mind within its wake.
For everyday tasks I'm reluctant,
my happiness and hopes, this event did take.

Maybe one day I'll truly smile again.
Maybe one day my guilt will subside.
But most likely what I'll do until then,
is crawl in my bed, under the sheets I will hide.

Replay

When you see something you can't erase,
when you feel something that can't be unfelt.
The only thing that can take its place,
is emptiness to cover the hand you've been dealt.

Your mind can do many miraculous things,
but it can also perpetuate anguish.
It can replay the most horrific scenes,
and in the process, my lights extinguish.

To feel life leave someone you unconditionally love,
is something I won't wish on my worst enemy.
Things I should've said but couldn't think of,
when time was dwindling in front of me.

To be strong is such a daunting task.
The promises I made, I promise I'll hold.
What I don't know is whether I'll ever move past,
that replay of that day, as it unfolds.

To Remember

I try to remember every small detail,
every word, every laugh, every moment.
I try to remember when you wouldn't let me fail,
and when you told me I needed to own it.

I try to remember the good not the bad,
you were so generous and kind,
I try to remember all the fun that was had,
the memories will never leave my mind.

My Stars

I decided to focus on the funny things,
because I truly didn't know where to start.
With all the events these past months bring,
emotions weigh heavy on these fragile hearts.

Now grandma you were by far a firecracker,
you had a way about you no one could deny.
All your grandchildren were whippersnappers,
and toes were threatened, my shakes alive.

Whether it was breakfast, dinner, or supper,
because in grandma's world dinner was twice,
all us hootie hoots came running, God help her,
get off the davenport, you'd chastise.

Your garden was not just a physical one,
you tended your family and helped us all grow.
Whether near or far, your work was never done,
look at the wonderful seeds your love did sew.

You were always blessing the world around you,
many heaven sakes and holy cows,
and lord have mercy you made it through,
by your britches I'm not sure how.

Oh and that holy mackerel was blessed everyday.
But truly now I must shake a leg before I fall apart,
the sadness that was previously at bay,
is slowly creeping back into the cracks of my heart.

It helps to know your joy is endless, your pain gone this time.
It comforts me to hear your music on the joyful organ above.
I can hear your laugh as you rest with your Father and mine.
Know that it won't be the same, without your enduring love.

Timely Tease

All things are right in their place,
the dust has settled anew.
I can finely embrace this happy face,
and put to rest the feelings of blue.

And just when I begin to think
there's nothing that can bring me down,
the world can change in a simple blink,
my smile morphing to a frown.

To say our timing was simply off
does no justice to things created.
If only the feelings could be enough,
to keep this union satiated.

There's always plenty of factors at play,
life pulling in every direction,
bombarding us every which way,
leaving behind the misconception.

Because once you find your sweet piece,
that little slice of lovely heaven,
You realize what a horrible tease,
this world is, that we now dwell in.

Crying World

The sky is falling, viciously down pouring.
My heart is breaking, the world is mourning.
To you, Lord, I am imploring.
You have maimed me, I am informing.

The pain of loss is indescribable.
My soul completely unrecognizable.
My happiness unreliable.
The sadness looming is undeniable.

Why is the question so often asked.
The sinking line has been cast.
Life is changing oh so fast.
I felt at first, but now I'm last.

Constantly wailing is my world inside.
But there is no place to quickly hide.
To those I'm close to, I confide.
Waiting, wishing, the pain subside.

Father's Day

I knew this day would be extremely sad,
it will always be from here on out.
It amplifies your absence Dad,
we are missing you without a doubt.

One less chair at the table,
One less "hey sweetie" today,
One less exaggerated fable,
One less hug my way.

One less…could go on forever,
I can't bring myself to list more.
Dad, I promise you that I'll never,
take for granted the 5, now 4.

-Love you Dad, Happy Father's Day in heaven.

Battles

Each day is a new battle.
I try not to get rattled.
I honestly don't want the fight,
I just want my heart to feel right.

My armor is starting to fray,
each attack, day by day.
I try to load my ammunition,
my worst fears coming to fruition.

Empty Whispers

The world has crushed the spirit within,
any shadow of potential no more.
The creativity of the mind gone dim,
paling in comparison to the fiery passion before.

The sad songs of dreams but whispers,
lost amongst ears that don't hear.
The excitement for adventure now drifters,
wandering aimlessly along a path unclear.

The desire to engage smothered by longst,
to wallow alone inside an empty shell.
The body now a trap for the soul amongst,
the dark thoughts that weave throughout this hell.

Fierce Love

For I have seen the meaning of commitment,
it's far beyond what it is today.
For I have seen this love transmitted,
through every action and word they say.

Because when something is truly this fierce,
there's nothing that can smother this flame.
This type of love can truly pierce,
anything that stands in its way.

From a simple touch or word unspoken,
a quick look or a thought unheard,
each task, every movement is a token,
of the union that occurred.

Injured Bird

Just as an injured bird is cast from its flock,
I too feel alone in the sky.
For a moment I sit and take stock,
of all the reasons and ask myself why.

Surrounded by clouds and trees abundant,
a forest teeming with life,
why does this cycle seem so redundant,
causing me all this pain and strife.

I close my eyes and flap my wings,
holding my breath as I leap,
thinking these all must be just dreams,
I attempt to return to my lonely sleep.

A Moment

For just a moment I felt much more.
For just a moment I opened the door.
I felt the passion once again,
praise the lord, amen, amen!

For but it was just a quick blink.
For but it was just....I think.
To my dismay the smile gone,
just as quickly as the dawn.

Hide and Seek

To some it may seem but a simple game,
people hide and then they're found.
We only have ourselves to blame,
just be quiet, make no sound.

Just be you, but change all you wear.
Just be you, but restyle your hair.
Just be you, but maybe fix your face.
Just be you, but know your place.
Just be you, but not so tall.
Just be you, but not you at all.

To some it may seem you have nothing to say.
They only see what they feel is right.
You must hide your tongue or they may,
reject what they see when there is the light.

To feel, alone but be amongst friends.
To feel, your decisions are knives on both ends.
To feel, wrong about something so right.
To feel, you must hide what should be in plain sight.
To feel, no one will accept the truth be told.
To feel, condemned and your soul resold.

To some their world is smaller than belief,
they don't understand because they don't know,
they don't ever ask nor do they seek,
the knowledge, the apple, that something, to grow.

Pieces of Me

There is a burning energy inside,
this fuel, this fire, I cannot hide,
I feel unfulfilled I must confide,
I stray from the path I once relied.

I move amongst the stones so slow,
to where I move I do not know,
I feel a pull, a nagging flow,
a force that grows no matter where I go.

I search for meaning all the time,
I even search within this rhyme,
I find that there is no clear sign,
to guide my feet as I decline.

I stumble upon a simple piece,
I find it's place to my relief,
and then these shackles I release,
but the feeling does not cease.

So the journey continues on,
parts of me just scattered gone,
now my part is to play a pawn,
when do I waken to the dawn.

The Veil

Simply a cloth to cover this face,
to hide the true nature within.
The sadness that is holding this space,
even to this, I've become akin.

And so I step forward unwilling,
a force I attempt to control,
the dread of this unveiling,
completely consuming my soul.

To try and be something you're not,
it takes all the energy inside.
I know with no veil I'll be caught,
on this darkness, I've relied.

Summer Shell

Like a singular shell by the sea,
lonely as can be.
Sitting and waiting for no reason,
existing for the season.

Many a person will wander by,
on the waves I rely,
to sweep me somewhere I belong,
as life continues right along.

The Best Intentions

I try to do these things with the best of intention,
but all I produce is a wealth of contention.
Every word I say leaves my breath in suspension,
my last chance at verbal redemption.

I try to avoid the triggers with honest resolution,
though impossible I search for a solution.
The differences are simply a constant involution,
the more they turn, the more the pollution.

The air remains thick with an intolerable density,
the problems remain with impending immensity.
Despite our desires, our thoughts drip with propensity,
to fight for our belief with enormous intensity.

To try is only to fail once again a constant defeat.
How do I get this sad song off repeat?
Alas, I now realize the only route for our meet,
I will just stand here and stare at my feet.

Other Life

To dream of a life so different than mine,
what form, what places does this dream take.
The thought sounds so simply divine,
to choose different with the choices that I did make.

To dream of the freedom that a life beyond could give,
outside of the four white walls I now inhabit.
What kind of life is this one that I currently live,
To have a chance to leave, be with those I love, I'd grab it.

Balancing Scale

With just one addition it tips to the side,
my life now slides in that direction.
I add more to compensate for the ride,
but now I am off center, imperfection.

Every time I attempt a proper adjustment,
some addition or subtraction arrives.
Everything I add of value faces judgment,
what doesn't measure up, doesn't survive.

So much weight to ensure the quality of time,
how much energy is put into each decision.
The pressure weighs more than this scale of mine,
each second wasted, is one required for revision.

Rocks

I can feel the weight, compressing in on both sides.
I'm not sure how to choose which one to push.
My sanity, on this decision, relies,
if I don't do something, I'll soon be squished.

The rock of grief compels me to cry once again.
It's a solid foundation for my sorrow.
It makes me feel I have no right to smile when
something brings me joy, I dispel 'til tomorrow.

The rock of life forces me to embrace the present.
It's dense interior leaving no space for pain.
It makes me feel as if I should be more pleasant,
pursuing my dreams, dancing in the pouring rain.

Between these two pressures, how can it be done?
How can I choose, I need one to have the other.
The force that drives both is simply the same one.
The inner critic rock is here, I can't handle another.

Divine Intervention

Most people ask for help from above when faced with a trial,
I prayed, I searched, that's exactly what I tried to do Lord.
But I struggle with understanding your plan, I'm in denial,
you have control and when you made it rain, it truly poured.

I thought maybe after some time I could come visit you again,
but the feeling of betrayal weighed heavy on this soul.
You have always been there to catch me when I fall, Amen,
but where were you when I began to fall down a gaping hole.

I am torn between wanting to love you and hating for taking,
even though I guess nothing is really mine in this world.
Why wouldn't you take something else, avoid heart breaking,
instead you took the best of the best, my mind tossed, swirled.

How could you make me but allow damage that breaks me?
I am just trying to make sense of how you pick and choose.
The battle within never ending right now, I'm blind, can't see,
I really need to know God, why do some win and others lose?

There are so many thoughts as I walk past your holy place,
there's a pull, yearning, I hope light enters by divine osmosis.
I have an appetite, hunger for the food offered, I need a taste,
or I feel I may whither away, starve, fade, that's my prognosis.

In the Clouds

I would rather be floating through the puffy clouds,
on this unforgiving day.
I'd rather......anything at all,
anything to keep these feelings far at bay.

I would rather be hopping from cirrus to stratus,
plucking the air like cotton candy.
I'd rather be finding shapes,
bunnies, turtles, what have you, just dandy.

I would rather be dodging the lightning from nimbus,
sticking my tongue out for the rain,
catching the drops....my tears.
No matter the distraction, I return to my pain.

Sometimes I can't

Sometimes I can't get out of this bed,
sometimes I can't get out of my head.
Sometimes it takes everything in me,
sometimes there's nothing to give, forgive me.

Sometimes there's no explanation,
sometimes I just feel my resignation.
Sometimes there are no words to describe,
sometimes the letters are pushed to the side.

Sometimes all I think about is escape,
sometimes I need to get away from this place.
Sometimes I feel all the feels,
sometimes it just doesn't feel real.

Sometimes I'd rather not be here,
sometimes I hope for a better year.
Sometimes I think, what's the point,
sometimes I wish I didn't disappoint.

Sometimes I'd like to press rewind,
sometimes I already feel behind.
Sometimes I want to just move ahead,
sometimes I can't get out of this bed.

Gift of Life

Like a breeze on the beach
so life passes each time.
An energy that can't be reached,
not even through this rhyme.

Another soul full of love,
pain now familiar to my core,
not lost, simply gifted above,
another wave, on this dismal shore.

Gardens Galore

I knew this was an inevitable day.
I knew that my hug, our words were the last.
I knew it would be difficult with what to say.
I knew you'd want to be with Grandma fast.

To be able to share in your stories of long ago.
To be able to partake in your travel dreams.
To be able to see you smile, I know.
To be able to cherish these special things.

I know you now have pain no more.
I know you now can truly breathe.
I know you now have gardens galore.
I know that now I can finally grieve.

The Cloak

Even though most think they see me,
not too many know who I really am.
Some may even wish to be me,
but few will truly understand.

For as I roam my complex world,
so I wear a different cloak.
Home is where I come unfurled,
I finally let my shield just soak.

It hides me when my face may fail,
and gets dirty from each space I go.
Sometimes it tears if I snag a nail,
I always have some thread to sew.

It's become a comfort to have at hand,
provides me with courage when I want to run.
It becomes my blanket on the sand,
my shelter from the scorching sun.

I have begun to experiment with my fear,
I've left my door with cloak in bag.
But the moment I sense danger near,
I unfold my trusty rag.

Lonely Island

I became so accustomed to the feeling of belonging,
all the pieces just so simply fell into their place.
That when I first felt the burn of isolation, the scalding,
my confusion must have been evident on my face.

It took the breath from my lungs, the wind from my sails,
my heart shattered with the realization, the dynamic shifted.
My vacant stare as my inner demons became a startling wail,
my core shaken, I disappeared, I became small, I drifted.

There are moments I feel who I was return to the present,
I can feel the energy begin to emerge, the laughter in my voice,
but all it takes is that small shift, here I am, again unpleasant,
isolation creeping into my roots, feeding, fueling my choice.

I feel alone in my grief, deserted by the company of emotion,
abandoned even by the anger that I clung to so desperately.
Seeking, grasping for a light to help rekindle some devotion,
attempting to find commonality, rebuild, but do so separately.

I fall short every time, I keep reaching but grasp no hand.
So many offers, much love has been thrown my way if I could,
I would hold each moment, capture them quick like sand,
filling the desert I built, voids filling the place I once stood.

Choices

In one second our whole life changes.
In one decision our course of action shifts.
The median of where we were now ranges,
in one minute time freezes with rifts.

In that flash of a moment all is a question.
In what way will this butterfly effect present.
In one hour what will my emotions be dressed in,
in one day what choices will I resent.

The Pain of Pain

Only pain can inflict the most brutal of all pains that exist.
Everyone handles it differently but when broken down,
those that wreak havoc on happiness often enlist,
the most tragic of memories to fuel their frown.

To find love in the coldest of places, the pure starkness,
to meet desperation with a heart of giving is no easy task,
to find compassion when all some may see, is darkness,
it will take all the patience that one could ask.

Most can't see beyond their own pain, blinded by grief,
they are moving amongst shadows, in the dark, they grope.
Their walls built so high that no one could possibly reach,
many think they want company but what they need is hope.

Hope in knowing they aren't alone, a feeling familiar to most.
The whispers of doubt are heard by many ears in the crowd,
a desire to fade away into the air we breathe, become a ghost,
the constant looming of the rain, a storm, a cloud.

If we could but recognize that common thread,
meeting each pain with the face of recognition,
leaving some words that shouldn't be said,
growing understanding within the omission.

Motions

I simply move in a direction.
My body just going through the motions.
My mind vacant of an specific selection.
My heart void of any particular devotions.

There's no choice in the matter.
No desire to choose even if there was.
To be gone or here, I guess I'd choose the latter.
Is it really significant, what one does?

My mouth moves but emptiness creeps out,
nothing of value is contributed to the conversation.
My anguish, hidden by softer sadness no doubt,
my apathetic nature impeding any relation.

To feel alone amongst many others,
it must be the true definition of isolation.
To choose to be alone simply smothers,
any attempt at happiness, acceleration.

Ciao Pescao

Cuando te conocí, estaba custodiada.
No sabía como ver más allá de mis paredes.
Todavía lucho por subir y estoy cansada,
y aquí, si puedo subir con una escalera, si se puede.

A veces estoy perdida en mi mente,
se necesita una persona paciente para despertarme.
A veces me pierdo entre la gente,
y solo necesito uno mano para encontrarme.

La chispa de la vida todavía en mi cuerpo.
Puedo sentir la llama dentro de mi corazón.
No quiero que este momento llegue, es cierto.
Porque una vez que te vas, estoy sola, adiós mi pasión.

Church Bells

I sit here in a sea of sorrow amongst others,
each with their own pain, joy, or mystery.
Everyone has lost love; sons, friends, and mothers,
do I now relate more to their history?

I've been here before but don't recognize this place.
A wilderness of prayer and praise in which I can't partake.
My body, my mind, simply a waste of space.
My pain and my anger are all that's left in my wake.

Constantly tossed between wanting to love, placing the blame.
Moments of clarity emerge, my indignation, I must refrain.
Then another minute of clarity where grace is your name,
my constant fluctuation and internal battle has me insane.

I try to comprehend what the preacher's message may be,
so I sit back down after the song and return to pondering fate.
I reach for the bible, open the book, find a verse for me,
it says if we keep pain long enough, we become what we hate.

To Feel, To Not Feel

Just like the game from my childhood flower,
I pull each petal to find an answer.
To think an inanimate object has that kind of power,
to think the world might possibly grant her.

A dilemma that is confusing upon itself.
To feel what I feel, but what is not feeling,
simply picking away at my feelingless wealth,
the feeling of lack of feeling has me reeling.

But alas, why don't I reframe my mindset.
A flower is a flower, living and surviving.
The same as my soul, far from done yet.
Seeking some light so I can switch to thriving.

The List of Things

And just when you think it's terminated,
you've finally finished, so elated,
another thing pops into your head,
then another, and again, again, I'm dead.

This constant cycle of futility,
it's finally formed a novel disability,
and to even simply prioritize,
is just another addition, in my eyes.

To ask when it ends is a pointless endeavor,
that list will just go on and on forever.
How does one who struggles with coping,
overcome the concept of hollow hoping.

Is the answer as simple as losing a pen?
Won't that list just form in my mind again?
What could possibly be the justification,
for this feeling of bulleted suffocation.

Why does the world have me feeling compelled,
to even think a list like this can be upheld.
The real problem isn't the list at all, re-spun,
the problem is, we base our worth on if it gets done.

Destiny

Obligations
are choice less dedications,
a force against
commenced.

Predetermined,
destiny's latest sermon,
the present taken,
forsaken.

Relinquished,
all dreams vanquished,
standing stunned,
shunned.

Cover Me

And like the darkness that has loomed over me,
so the dreaded veil covers my soul.
I have denied acknowledging this daily,
but here it confronts and grabs ahold.

A part of me will be forever dead and floating at sea,
never to return no matter how hard I search.
I understand you will never really abandon me,
but in truth, the lack of your physical being hurts.

With boundless love from family and friends around,
all here to celebrate a life once flourishing,
how can one like myself feel lost while found,
as I sit here, not understanding, simply wishing.

So I lift the veil,
pay the toll,
again I fail,
my darkened soul.

A Spark

And just as a fire may start,
so begins my heart.
A slow process to flame,
the heat the same.

I had attempted prior,
but alas no fire.
A new beginning is key,
keep trying, it may be.

Control

My plans have always been out of my hands.
I try to control it all but to no avail.
Control is all relative and can't withstand,
the constant variations that appear to derail.

To relinquish control of my mouth is hard to pronounce.
Considering the words of a crusader.
To secede control of my heart would renounce,
the walls I have built to prevent an invader.

Why do we feel we have any power?
How can we feel our choices are ours?
I refuse to hide in my corner and cower.
I cannot stand by to count, countless hours.

I simply need to accept this place, but here I vow,
acceptance by no means is a closing door.
The time to control has passed for now,
but it's evident that soon I'll be seeking more.

You see if all else in my life is decrepit,
if I have no say in my situation,
then my acceptance is simply my method,
to gain control of this renovation.

Who Am I

I am, someone.

I have dreams, and desires that permeate every part of my body and soul.

I feel, so deeply, in every capacity, in every part of my heart, within every role.

I hear, the things people aren't saying because I listen to more than just their words.

I want, to experience the joy of floating amongst the clouds, the type of freedom only reserved for the birds.

I see, beyond the concrete possibilities of life and strive to explore the impossible.

I know, my head is always exploding with ideas and dreams, I truly feel are plausible.

I realize, I'm always late but it's only because I want to make the most of each day.

I have, I feel, I hear, I see, I know, I realize. I am someone, I say.

And so it goes...

And so time continues on passing,
even though I feel as though it's suspended.
The world keeps turning, people keep laughing,
but I still feel my world upended.

Your life, your story, beginning and end,
it stopped so abruptly, everything else kept going.
How do I reconcile what I can't comprehend,
everything is rolling, even my tears keep flowing.

There's so much still you needed to see,
so many lives you needed to save.
Why isn't everyone feeling this pain with me,
each day I become more of its slave.

Two Places

How can I feel two places in one?
How can there be peace at war?
Is it possible to burn with no sun,
to win if no one keeps score.

Is it possible to bloom between two rocks,
to have that pressure on both sides.
Is it possible to live by these clocks,
to navigate this world amongst all these guides.

Is it possible to be both sweet and sour.
How can my head be spinning while my body is still.
How can I yield so much power,
but still be held against my will.

Is it possible to be drunk on pain,
even though you've avoided the glass.
How can you dance in the rain,
if you've never taken a dancing class.

So there you have it, a world of two.
Both things can exist despite protest.
You can be sad and want happy within the blue,
you can still find serenity amongst unrest.

Myself

By now I should.
Shouldn't I?
I should know.
Don't I?

To know yourself.
I do.
But it's difficult.
It is.

There is much to consider.
It's complicated.
Always learning.
Indefinite growth.

But the core remains.
It's true.
At the core.
It's you.

Dirty Laundry

My heart tumbles around like dirty clothes,
waiting for someone to wash it clean.
The dirt and grime may stain I suppose,
not really wanting the filth to be seen.

The cycle just keeps going and going,
when will the buzzer make it all stop.
I think the turmoil is finally showing,
the laundry has finally reached the top.

Back Down

Through the sorrow I have built my back up.
Through my vulnerability I have softened my front.
Through all the odds that may stack up,
I know my will and strength can bear the brunt.

Another part of life we always will encounter,
are those who pull into question our worth.
They force us to defend our integrity with a counter,
but no longer will I stand trial for my time on earth.

You see I now know my power,
I know exactly who I am.
I no longer cower,
for this I take a stand.

At first my life was hanging by a thread,
my sanity and confidence weighing down that delicate string.
Through much hard work on my soul which soon led
me to realize some wonderful and beautiful things.

I had been talking but was not heard.
I had been walking with fear of breaking eggs under my feet.
I had been trapped in belief and lies absurd.
I had been shamed by my own defeat.

You see I know who I am.
It's instilled in my core.
I will no longer backdown,
hear my courage, feel my roar.

Lonely Heart

Heartbreak is more than just a broken part,
it's more than just simply being sad.
Deep heartache means you're a world apart,
from the person this world once had.

It means that whenever you may come across,
happiness in unions you see nearby,
a feeling of envy in your heart will toss,
and then the guilt you feel will make you cry.

The longing we feel for the love that has no place,
that's the true havoc that damages from the start.
It wanders about in heaven or maybe in space,
while we fumble with wear to place our lonely heart.

Birthday

Today is a day that's meant for rejoice,
and I would celebrate if I had the choice.
There are times I laugh as I recall,
you not wanting presents at all.

You really never asked for much,
simply wanting a future and such.
And on this day, I'll try to make you proud,
I think that present should be allowed.

All the gifts in the world I would give,
just to have you simply live.
So on this birthday I will laugh and cry,
hoping you're reading from the sky.

Free Spirit

And like a flash through the crashing waves,
joyful skips from childhood days,
laughter amidst the ocean symphony,
their free spirits mingle sinfully.

And like a fresh breath for a bubble to blow,
their happiness comes from deep below,
they hail as a sign from way above,
their playful ways filled with love.

Old Life

What to do.
What do you need?
Please stop crying.
Please, please, please.

I'm going on two,
Maybe even less.
How did I get here?
What a complete mess.

Just a day ago
I felt I was flying.
Traveling the world,
now I'm standing here crying.

The world has gone,
a new one has come.
I want it all back......
even just some.

I had no care,
could go grab coffee.
I chose for me,
no goal was too lofty.

I didn't think,
I only would move.
I laughed at settling.
I had nothing to prove.

Nothing's ever right.
Everyone has a say.
But it's my child,
It should be my way?

Doesn't matter,
here I stand,
old life gone,
bottle in hand.

But then you stop,
You stare up at me.
You make it all worth it,
This new life that I see.

Just Say It

My words stumbling and falling,
tripping and jumbling as they cascade.
Talking obviously not my calling,
my phrases lining up, a messy parade.

No time for anything in between,
it seems so simple to just say.
Simply say what you mean,
and then actually mean what you say.

In my head it makes sense,
but somewhere along a path inside,
things get caught in the fence,
and every word seems to collide.

Maybe I need to inhale and exhale,
I need to simply breathe.
Peacefully like a blissful tale,
slowly let the words just leave.

The Biggest Fear

Some people fear the idea of death,
some fear things they can't reveal,
some fear seeing one's last breath,
some fear what they can't unfeel.

But after a fear comes to fruition,
after the worst stares you in the face,
after losing faith in your intuition,
after feeling unsafe in your safe space.

What can truly strike a real fear?
Everything else just seems so small.
Even the worst pain is welcome here.
Maybe a fear, is not having any, at all.

Glasses

I stare blankly at my wine.
Glass half full, empty, gone.
My sight perfectly fine,
my hand a puppet, a pawn.

Clarity is so subjective and evasive,
blended red, white, rose.
Really seeing is actually invasive,
another glass, what do you say.

Dreams and Reasons

Bombarded with the hustle of life,
we tend to set aside what drives us.
What gives us purpose, builds the hype,
our dreams, to our hearts we entrust.

But then there's always tomorrow, right?
Something always takes priority.
Until we willfully decide to keep in sight,
until we decide with definite authority.

No one will give us the right reason,
because only we know what drives this force.
Any challenge we face is just a season,
our minds the fuel, our hearts the source.

Forgiving the Guilty

Like a scab that is reopened again,
and again the betrayal.
an unspoken sin,
guilt for the win.

To forgive others much easier than me,
we replay the record over,
and over to see,
the cost not free.

Constant shame is difficult to pass,
keeps returning with no remorse,
recycling so fast,
reliving the past.

Priceless

Everything moving so fast around me,
it's like I'm in slow motion.
Watching but not understanding.
Trying to grasp, but not withstanding.

Then a pause in the air around me,
the fleeting moment passes.
But in that brief second my heart,
it stops, some clarity, that's a start.

Trying to calm the chaos within me,
I sometimes surround myself with it.
But the solution is more than phrases,
more than thoughts, more than phases.

Searching deep, further inside me,
I must stay present, looking forward.
Staying positive more difficult than I thought,
if only time could be bought.

Wise Eyes

The search for meaning is never ending,
and as we age it becomes essential.
Some search by continuous over spending,
while others attempt to fulfill potential.

What we seek now we may later regret,
but if we can learn from what we find,
life will not be wasted just yet,
and maybe we won't feel so left behind.

Someone once asked me my life's lesson,
thus far there have been many times of teaching.
The one thing I find to be a blessing,
is that my body will always be reaching.

My eyes will always look with compassion,
my hands will always be offered for assistance,
my heart will always be filled with passion,
my feet will always conquer resistance.

My ears will always be available to listen,
my mind will always try to find a solution,
my soul will always flow freely on a mission,
my gift will be offered as sincere restitution.

You see it's not what life can offer up to us,
it's what we can offer to the living.
Our legacy isn't something we can touch,
have you decided how you'll be giving?

ACKNOWLEDGEMENTS

Front cover photo skills by *Lauren Luiz*
Ice cream runs and pure patience by *Tyler Thompson*
Cover photo editing by *Briana Ditlove*
Cover format and design by *Melissa Means*
Cover format and design edits by *Dave Ahmad*
Pet therapy provided by the best puppies, *Max and Angel*
Random poetry readings supported by *Camilla Sawick*

And many other friends and family who have supported me in every way, along the way; I could not have completed this without you.

ABOUT THE AUTHOR

Annalisa Sawick

Annalisa Sawick is originally from Chicago, graduated from University of Iowa in 2009 with her Bachelor of Science in Psychology, then in 2014 received her Master of Science from Mount Mary University in Wisconsin. After years of wanting to be in warm weather, she decided to head out to the west coast; living in places like San Diego and LA while pursuing a career in Travel Occupational Therapy. Life had its ups and downs, businesses were started and failed, lots of lessons were learned, but her biggest hurdle was yet to come.

With her father's passing in May of 2019, she decided to be near her mother who resided in southern Florida. Soon after, the family experienced the loss of their grandmother and grandfather as well. Using poetry as her outlet for pain and grief, the writing began to develop into more than just words on paper. She soon realized that her writing could actually help others; life was too short to keep a gift hidden. She had promised her Dad that she would publish her work and she was not about to break that promise because of fear. And so begins her newest adventure yet, with her pup Max, pursuing her passion of writing while she embraces the plan that was so imperfect it became unexpectedly perfect.

Made in the USA
Columbia, SC
01 September 2020